FLOWERY THOUGHTS

NATIONAL LIBRARY OF AUSTRALIA

A catalogue record for this book is available from the National Library of Australia

Published 2022

ISBN: 978-0-6454300-0-4 (epub)
ISBN: 978-0-6454300-1-1 (paperback)
ISBN: 978-0-6454300-2-8 (hardcover)

9 780645 430011

Published with the aid of Jumble Books and Publishers
(https://jumblebooksandpublishers.com)

flowery thoughts

Joan Whitehead

ABOUT THE AUTHOR

Born and raised in the UK, Joan now lives in Western Australia, where she runs her own art and craft gallery and studio, creating and selling her own work.

She has always enjoyed creating things, from paintings and jewellery to glass work and books.

She is pleased to have had five books published in the past; the first one being a craft book, followed by four children's picture story books.

Another of her interests has always been writing rhymes and poems. She hopes you will find them interesting also.

CONTENTS

THE BUMBLE BEE 2

LIFE 4

THE STORM 6

SONG OF THE SEA 8

THE DARK 10

SHARK..12

LOVE'S SONG 14

DREAMING...16

UNICORN 18

ONE RAINDROP 20

SEEDS 22

FORGET-ME-NOT 24

NATURE'S MAGIC 26

SPRING 28

DAISY DREAMS..30

A NEW DAY 32

NATURE'S WAY 34

THE FROG SONG 36

FLOWERS...38

GARDENING...40

THE WISHING WELL 42

THE MIGHTY OAK 44

THE BUMBLE BEE

Life can be just like a

Bumble Bee.

You gather honey

wherever you can see.

Roses, Poppies,

Geraniums and Clover.

Then back to the hive,

to start all over.

<u>LIFE</u>

Life is what you make of it

wishing doesn't make it so.

Plant the seed and water it.

Then sit back and watch it grow.

Some people have sunshine.

Some people have rain.

Some people have happiness

Some people have pain.

It's up to the gods, your fate to choose.

Heads you win, tails you lose.

Play the game, toe the line.

Hope everything will work out fine.

Dream your dreams, sing your song.

No matter if it's right or wrong.

So, search for the sunshine.

Shelter from the rain.

Delight in all the happiness.

And forget about the pain.

To the gods and their plans, we will refuse.

Heads you win, tails you lose.

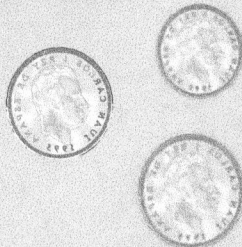

THE STORM

Autumn is here, down

comes the rain.

Although we do,

we shouldn't complain.

Lightning flashes

thunder roars

rain falls down,

it simply pours.

The storm passes by,

its course, its run.

Everything sparkles

and shines in the sun.

Rain is welcome

to the flowers below,

without the rain they

could not grow.

SONG OF THE SEA

The ocean roars,

it's the song of the sea.

The crashing waves,

they beckon to me.

The soapy surf whispers

of things far away.

Come play with us,

it seems to say.

Play in the waves,

splash with glee.

And the ocean roars,

it's the song of the sea.

<u>THE DARK</u>

The candlelight flickers

making shadows on the wall.

Did I hear voices,

out in the hall.

Whispering voices,

when no one is there.

Opening the door quietly.

With care,

I carry the candle.

One speck of light

Then with a breath of wind,

all is night.

<u>SHARK</u>

Silky smooth as it

slides on by.

Looking out of a

cold black eye.

With teeth of white,

and skin of grey.

Without a noise,

it stalks its prey.

One glance brings

a feeling of dread.

As slowly it turns

its massive head.

Should I flee,

or should I stay.

Or run, to fight another day.

LOVE'S SONG

If wishes were horses
even beggars would ride.

I've been wishing and hoping
now it's all cast aside.

Looking for a rainbow, to find
that pot of gold.

Wishes sometimes come true.

Or so I've been told.

Until then I'll look for that
songbird

and listen for his song

Hoping one day my love

will come along.

DREAMING

Waking from my slumbers,

I climb out of bed.

Visions of my dreams still running

through my head.

Soaring through the clouds,

way up in the sky.

Looking over land with an

Eagle's eye.

Running in the grass, so lush

and oh, so green.

Resting by the water of a cool

sparkling stream.

The visions start to fade, lost

in the light of day.

Lost until that night, in my bed

I once more lay.

<u>UNICORN</u>

Fairies and Elves and spiritual souls

Adrift on the air until twilight

unfolds.

The coming

of dawn,

life's new

beginning.

Wishes of love with hearts all
a'ringing.

So run little Unicorn down life's way.

With hope for the future and every
day.

ONE RAINDROP

Tell me, can one raindrop raise the ocean?

Can two hearts beat as one?

With love so strong, full of devotion

without it, can life go on?

Tell me, can one raindrop raise the ocean?

I'm so sad now that we are apart

I still exist, going through

the motions.

Without love and without a

heart.

Tell me, can one raindrop raise the ocean?

Can I love again someday?

Can this heart of mine feel real emotion?

This I really hope and pray.

Tell me, can one raindrop raise the ocean?

SEEDS

The garden bed is

blank and bare,

without attention

and no care.

Give it love

and tiny seeds,

then out come the

flowers,

even

the weeds.

FORGET-ME-NOT

Like

the summer sky

bright and

blue.

The

Forget-me-not says

"I'll not forget

you."

NATURE'S MAGIC

Down in the woods

under the trees,

there's a croaking

of frogs and a

buzzing of bees.

Silver streams and

babbling brooks.

Fairy rings and shady nooks.

Lifting the spirits

and filling the air,

nature's music

is everywhere.

Listen to the music

it is all around,

there's even magic

there to be found.

<u>SPRING</u>

Spring is here full of

promise anew,

bringing forth blooms

of every colour and hue.

Just like the rainbow

up in the sky.

Setting the heart singing

like the birds on high.

DAISY DREAMS

Daisy dreams on

lazy days.

Down in the

meadow, drifting away.

Though in everyone's

life there's a few

rainy days.

Flowers can

chase those rain

clouds away.

Say it with flowers,

there's lots you can say,

even if it's only have

a nice day.

A NEW DAY

Nodding heads

full of dew,

under the sky

of shining blue.

The cows in the meadow come out to play, the night is over, it's a new day.

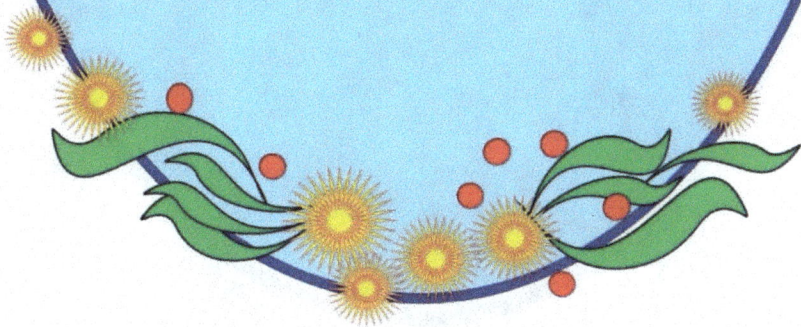

NATURE'S WAY

A mouse scurries by

out of sight.

The dawn is coming,

it's the end of the night.

The sun comes up

and greets a new day.

So life goes on,

Nature's way.

THE FROG SONG

The frog sits on the

Lily pad, he sings to

the moon ever so sad.

Tra la la, fiddle de de

here I am

poor lonesome me.

FLOWERS

Deep in the earth below,

the seeds are waiting

to grow.

There they lie

all winter through,

waiting for spring

to grow all anew.

Then up they come

trying to reach the sky,

flowers of every

colour to delight the eye.

The garden is

a magical place,

it can put a smile

on anyone's face.

__GARDENING__

Gardening is like

life, you reap what

you sow.

Friendship

and love are what you

should grow.

Grow them well,

strong and true,

then they will always

come back to you.

THE WISHING WELL

Deep in the forest

there's a secret dell,

therein lies a

wishing well.

Make a wish and

hope it comes true,

but be careful,

sometimes they do.

THE MIGHTY OAK

Deep as the ocean

high as the sky,

time is endless

as it flows on by.

Even the mighty

oak tree standing tall,

must wait for the

acorn to fall.

<u>Also by Joan Whitehead</u>

Step by step Transparent Art

Not Green

The Four Seasons of Sammy Snail

Piggy Tales*

Ten Ways to Please Your Mum*

* Coming soon